THE NEW DECADE SERIES

SONGS OF 1980s

🔊 81 Songs with Online Audio Backing Tracks

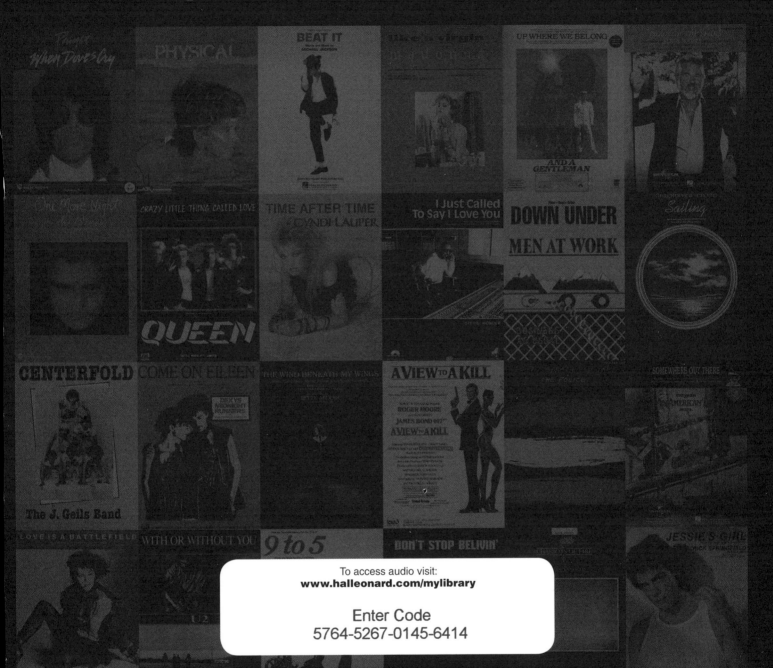

To access audio visit:
www.halleonard.com/mylibrary

Enter Code
5764-5267-0145-6414

ISBN 978-1-4950-0035-5

HAL•LEONARD®
CORPORATION
7777 W. BLUEMOUND RD. P.O. BOX 13819 MILWAUKEE, WI 53213

Visit Hal Leonard Online at
www.halleonard.com

ADDICTED TO LOVE

Words and Music by
ROBERT PALMER

ALL NIGHT LONG
(All Night)

Words and Music by
LIONEL RICHIE

ANGEL EYES

Words and Music by JOHN HIATT
and FRED KOLLER

Girl, ___ you're look - ing _____ fine _____ to - night, _
Well, I'm _____ the guy who nev - er learned _____ to dance. _
There's _ just one more thing ___ I need _____ to know: _

and ev - 'ry guy has _____ got you in _____ his sight. _
I nev - er e - ven _____ got one sec - ond glance. _
If this is love, why ___ does it scare _____ me so? _

What you're do - ing with a clown _____ like me _____
A - cross a crowd - ed room _____ was close _ e - nough. _
Must be some - thing on - ly you _____ can see, ___

ANOTHER BRICK IN THE WALL

Words and Music by
ROGER WATERS

We don't need_ no ed - u - ca - tion,
We don't need_ no ed - u - ca - tion,

We don't need_ no
We don't need_ no

thought con - trol,_
school con - trol,_

No
No

fade -- silence

BEAT IT

Words and Music by
MICHAEL JACKSON

They told him, "Don't you ev-er come a-round here. Don't wan-na see your face; you bet-ter
They're out to get you. Bet-ter leave while you can. Don't wan-na be a boy; you wan-na

dis-ap-pear." The fi-re's in their eyes and their words are real-ly clear. So
be a man. You wan-na stay a-live; bet-ter do what you can. So

CALL ME

from the Paramount Motion Picture AMERICAN GIGOLO

Words by DEBORAH HARRY
Music by GIORGIO MORODER

BILLIE JEAN

Words and Music by
MICHAEL JACKSON

CARELESS WHISPER

Words and Music by GEORGE MICHAEL
and ANDREW RIDGELEY

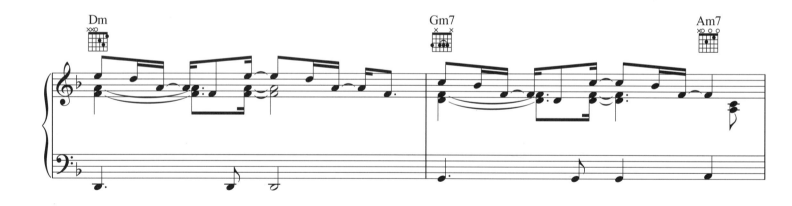

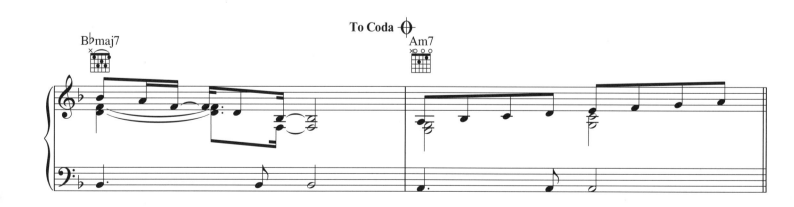

way I dance with you, oh.

To-

night the mu - sic seems so loud, I wish that we could lose this crowd,

may - be it's bet - ter this way, if we'd hurt each oth - er with the things we want to say. We

should have known bet - ter than to cheat a friend, _ and waste a chance that I've _ been giv - en,

so I'm nev - er gon - na dance a - gain _ the way I dance _ with you. _

Repeat ad lib. and Fade

CARIBBEAN QUEEN
(No More Love on the Run)

Words and Music by KEITH VINCENT ALEXANDER
and BILLY OCEAN

CENTERFOLD

Written by
SETH JUSTMAN

Bright Rock

Does she walk?__ Does she talk?__ Does she come com-plete?__ My
It's o-kay,__ I un-der-stand,__ this ain't no nev-er-nev-er land. I

home-room, home-room an-gel al-ways pulled me from my seat.
hope that when this is-sue's gone, I'll see you when your clothes are on.

CHARIOTS OF FIRE

By VANGELIS

Moderately

N.C.

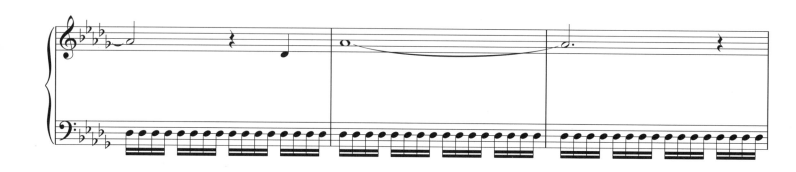

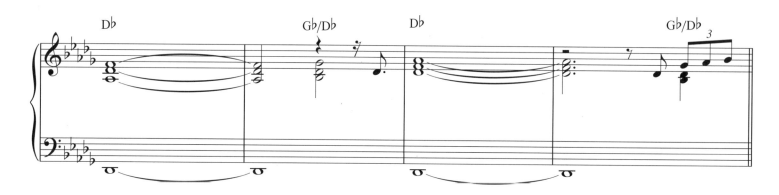

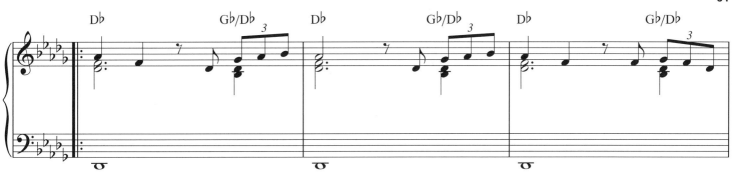

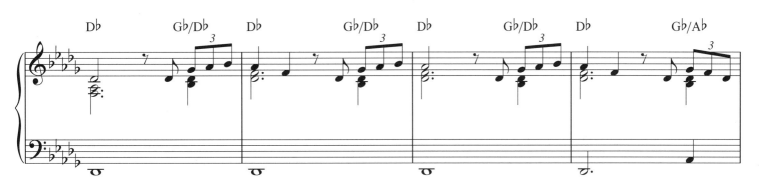

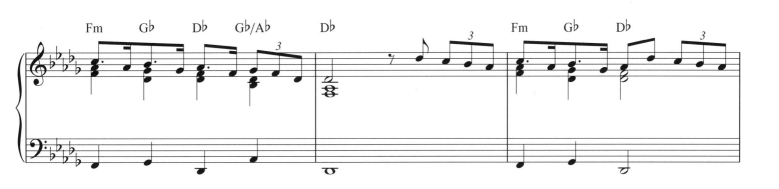

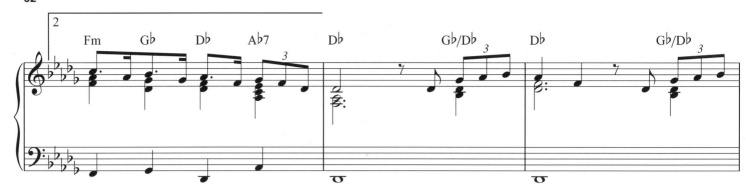

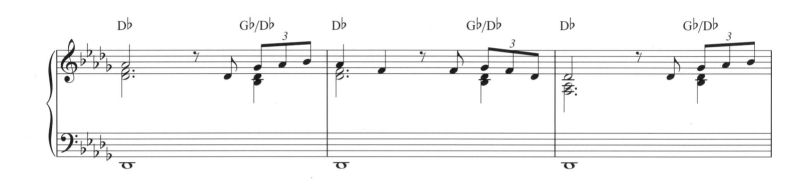

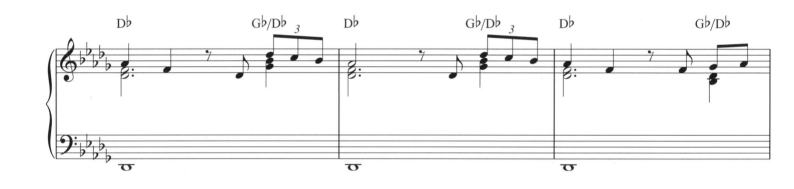

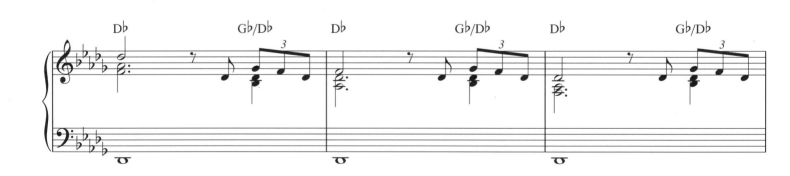

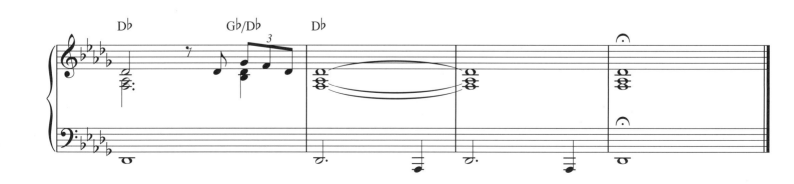

COME ON EILEEN

Words and Music by KEVIN ROWLAND,
JAMES PATTERSON and KEVIN ADAMS

CRAZY LITTLE THING CALLED LOVE

Words and Music by
FREDDIE MERCURY

Moderately fast Shuffle

Oh, this thing ___ called
___ called

love, well, I just ___ can't han - dle it. ___ This thing ___
love, it cries ___ in a cra - dle all night. It swings, ___

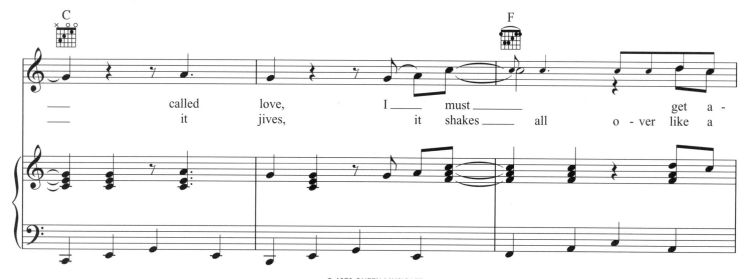

___ called love, I ___ must ___ get a -
___ it jives, it shakes ___ all o - ver like a

I got-ta be cool, ___ re - lax, ___

a - get hip, ___ a - get on my tracks. Take a

back seat, ___ hitch - hike ___ to take a lit - tle long_ ride_ on my

DOWN UNDER

Words and Music by COLIN HAY
and RON STRYKERT

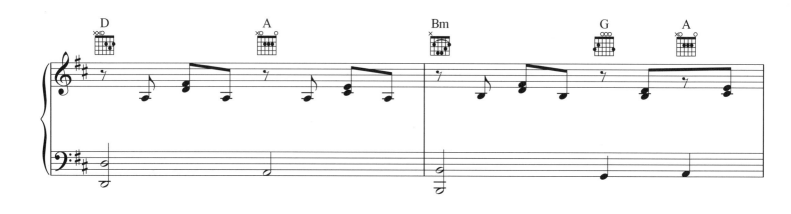

D.S. al Coda

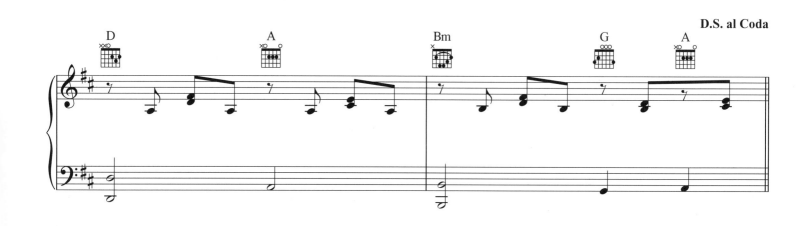

DON'T STOP BELIEVIN'

Words and Music by STEVE PERRY,
NEAL SCHON and JONATHAN CAIN

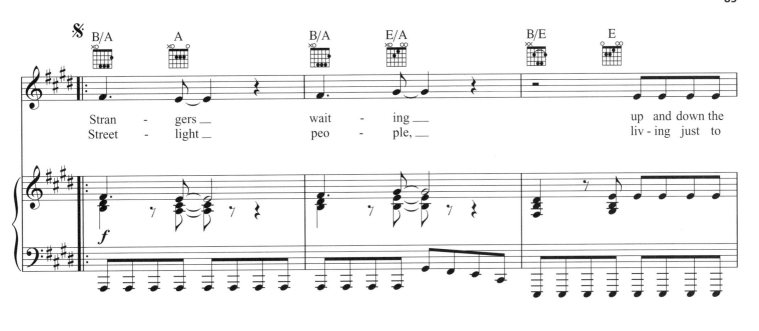

Stran - gers ___ wait - ing ___ up and down the
Street - light ___ peo - ple, ___ liv - ing just to

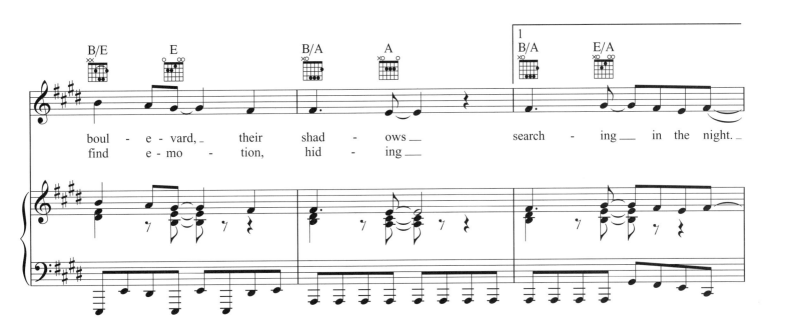

boul - e - vard, ___ their shad - ows ___ search - ing ___ in the night. ___
find e - mo - tion, hid - ing ___

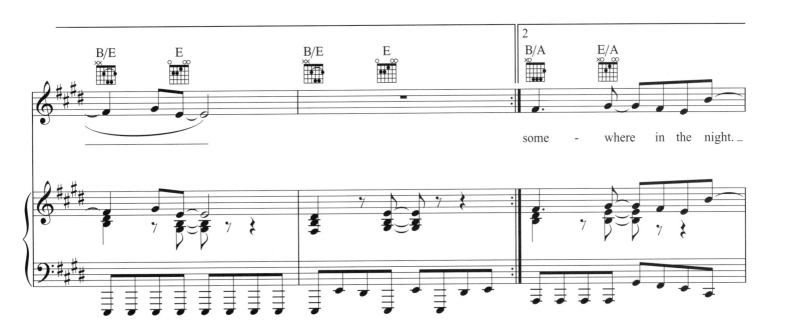

some - where in the night. ___

ENDLESS LOVE

Words and Music by
LIONEL RICHIE

Moderately slow

My love, there's on-ly you in my life,
Two hearts, two hearts that beat as one;

the on-ly thing that's right. My
our lives have just be-gun. For-

first love, you're ev-'ry breath that I take,
ev- er, I'll hold you close in my arms,

ESCAPE
(The Piña Colada Song)

Words and Music by
RUPERT HOLMES

Moderate groove

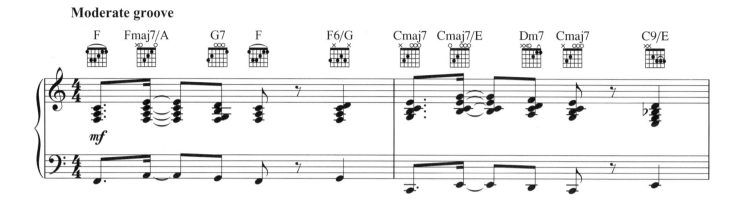

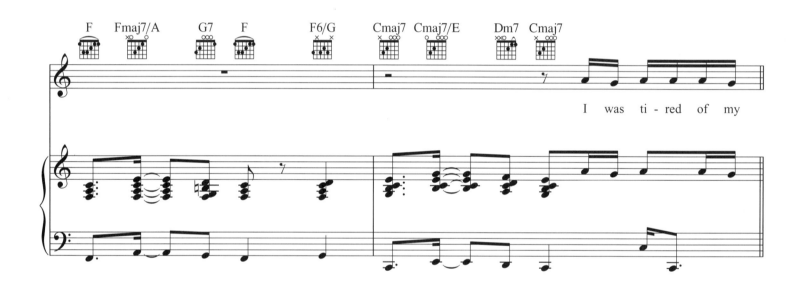

I was ti-red of my

la - dy,   we'd been to - geth - er too long. ___   Like a worn-out re-cord
la - dy,   I know I sound kind of mean. ___   But me and my old la-
hopes   and she walked in - to the place. ___   I knew her smile in an in-

-ing / -dy / -stant,

of my fa-vor-ite song. ___ / have fal-len in-to the same ___ old dull ___ rou-tine. ___ / I knew the curve of her face. ___

So while she lay there / So I wrote to the / It was my own love-ly

sleep-ing / pa-per, / la-dy,

I read the pa-per in bed. ___ / took out a per-son-al ad. ___ / and she said, "Oh, it's you." ___

And in the per-son-al col- / And though I'm no-bod-y's po- / Then we laughed for a mo-

-umns, / -et, / -ment,

there was this let-ter I read: ___ / I thought it was-n't half bad. ___ / and I said, "I nev-er knew ___

If you like pi-ña co- / Yes, I like pi-ña co- / that you liked pi-ña co-

la - das and get - ting caught in the rain, if you're not in - to
la - das and get - ting caught in the rain. I'm not much in - to
la - das, get - ting caught in the rain, and the feel of the

yo - ga, if you have half a brain,
health food, I am in - to cham - pagne.
o - cean and the taste of cham - pagne.

if you like mak - ing love at
I've got to meet you by to -
If you like mak - ing love at

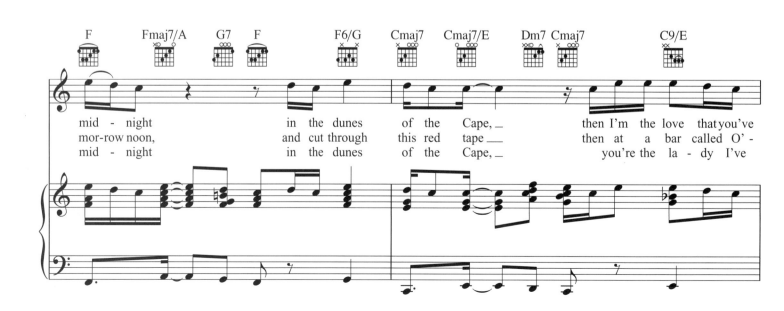

mid - night in the dunes of the Cape, __ then I'm the love that you've
mor - row noon, and cut through this red tape __ then at a bar called O' -
mid - night in the dunes of the Cape, __ you're the la - dy I've

EVERY BREATH YOU TAKE

Music and Lyrics by
STING

Moderate Rock

take,

ev-'ry move you__ make,

Ev-'ry breath you__

long for your _ em-brace. I keep cry - ing, ba - by, ba - by, please. _

EVERY ROSE HAS ITS THORN

Words and Music by BOBBY DALL,
C.C. DEVILLE, BRET MICHAELS
and RIKKI ROCKETT

We both lie si-lent-ly still __ in the dead of the night. __ Al-though we

both lie close to-geth-er, __ we feel miles a-part __ in-side. __ Was it

some-thing I said or some-thing I did? Did my words not come out right? __ Though I

lis- ten to our fa - v'rite song play- ing on the ra - di - o, _____ hear the

D. J. say love's a game of eas - y come and eas - y go. _____ But I

won- der does _ he know, has he ev - er felt _ like this? And I

111

EYE OF THE TIGER
Theme from ROCKY III

Words and Music by FRANK SULLIVAN
and JIM PETERIK

So man-y times __ it hap-pens too fast.
Face to face, __ out in the heat, __
Ris-in' up, __ straight to the top. __

You trade your pas - sion for glo - ry.
hang - in' tough, stay - in' hun - gry.
Had the guts, got the glo - ry.

Don't lose your grip __ on the
They stack the odds, __ still we

dreams of the past. You must fight just to keep them a - live. __
take to the street for the kill with the skill to sur - vive. __
not gon - na stop, just a man and his will to sur - vive. __

FLASHDANCE...WHAT A FEELING

from the Paramount Picture FLASHDANCE

Lyrics by KEITH FORSEY and IRENE CARA
Music by GIORGIO MORODER

122

FOOTLOOSE

Theme from the Paramount Picture FOOTLOOSE

Words by DEAN PITCHFORD
Music by KENNY LOGGINS

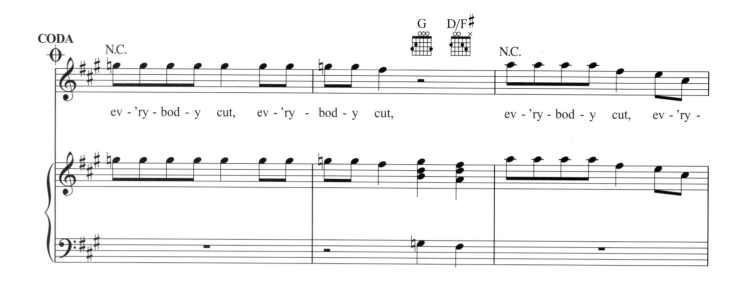

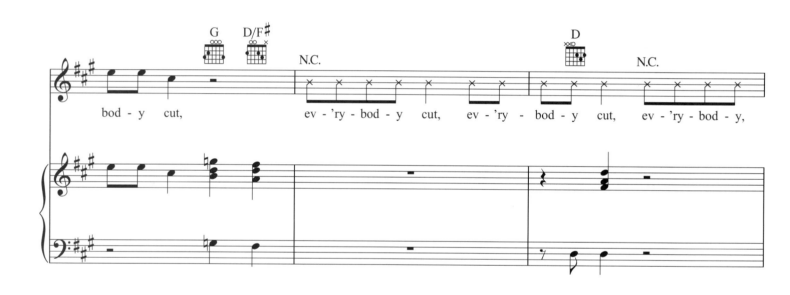

GOT MY MIND SET ON YOU

Words and Music by
RUDY CLARK

I got my mind set on you. I got my mind
set on you.

set on you. I got my mind set on you.
Set on you. I got my mind set on you.

Got my mind set on you. } But it's gon-na take mon-
Set on you.

GIRLS JUST WANT TO HAVE FUN

Words and Music by
ROBERT HAZARD

I come home in the morn - ing light. __ My moth-
The phone rings in the mid-dle of the night. My fa-
Some boys take a beau-ti-ful girl __ and hide __

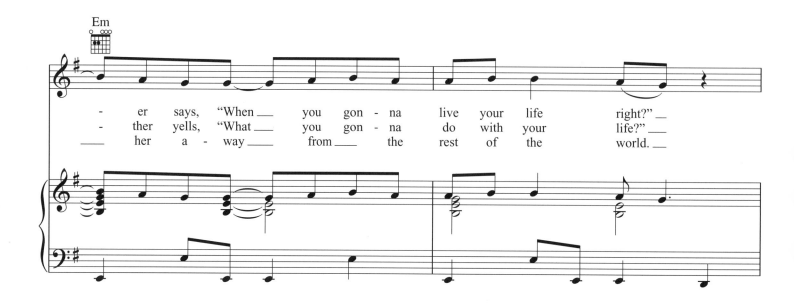

- er says, "When __ you gon - na live your life right?" __
- ther yells, "What __ you gon - na do with your life?" __
__ her a - way __ from __ the rest of the world. __

GLORY OF LOVE
Theme from KARATE KID PART II

Words and Music by DAVID FOSTER,
PETER CETERA and DIANE NINI

THE GREATEST LOVE OF ALL

Words by LINDA CREED
Music by MICHAEL MASSER

(1., D.S.) I be-lieve the chil-dren are our fu-ture;
be.(2.) Ev-'ry-bod-y's search-ing for a he-ro;

teach them well and let ___ them lead ___ the way.
peo-ple need some-one ___ to look up ___ to.

Show them all the beau-ty they pos-sess in-
I nev-er found an-y-one ___ who ful-filled my

HOW WILL I KNOW

Words and Music by GEORGE MERRILL,
SHANNON RUBICAM and NARADA MICHAEL WALDEN

* Cues 2nd time only

I LOVE A RAINY NIGHT

Words and Music by EDDIE RABBITT,
EVEN STEVENS and DAVID MALLOY

I JUST CALLED TO SAY I LOVE YOU

Words and Music by
STEVIE WONDER

Chorus

Additional Lyrics

3. No summer's high; no warm July;
   No harvest moon to light one tender August night.
   No autumn breeze; no falling leaves;
   Not even time for birds to fly to southern skies.

4. No Libra sun; no Halloween;
   No giving thanks to all the Christmas joy you bring.
   But what it is, though old so new
   To fill your heart like no three words could ever do.
   Chorus

I LOVE ROCK 'N ROLL

Words and Music by ALAN MERRILL
and JAKE HOOKER

Moderately

I saw him danc-ing there ___ by the rec-ord ma-
smiled, so I got up ___ and asked ___ for his

I STILL HAVEN'T FOUND WHAT I'M LOOKING FOR

Words and Music by
U2

Moderately, with a steady beat

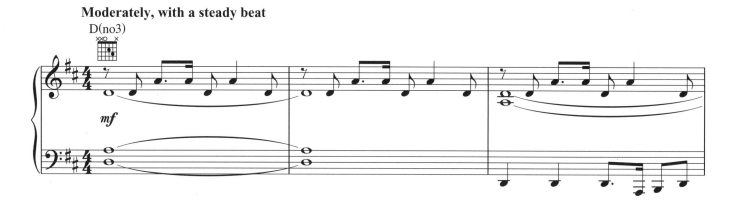

I have

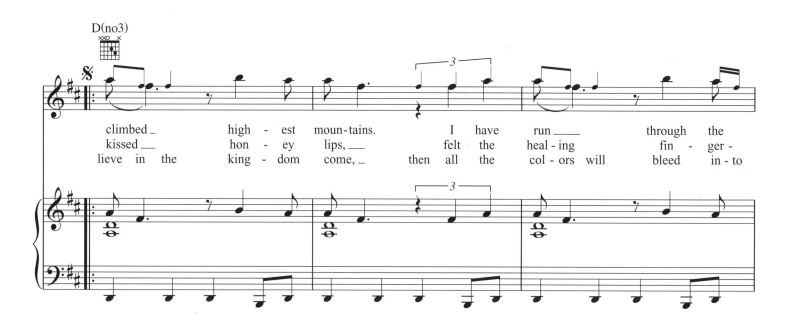

climbed ___ high - est moun - tains. I have run ___ through the
kissed ___ hon - ey lips, ___ felt the heal - ing fin - ger-
lieve in the king - dom come, ___ then all the col - ors will bleed in - to

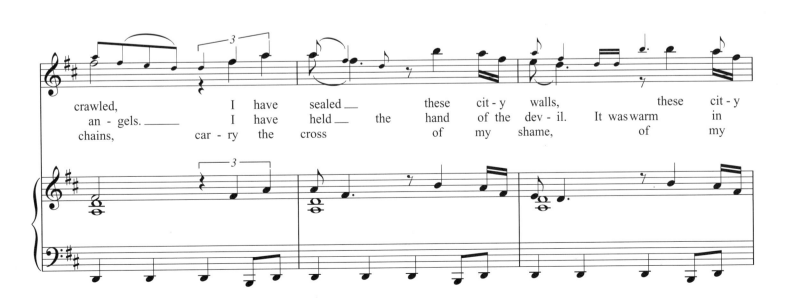

ISLANDS IN THE STREAM

Words and Music by BARRY GIBB,
ROBIN GIBB and MAURICE GIBB

IT'S STILL ROCK AND ROLL TO ME

Words and Music by
BILLY JOEL

Moderately fast

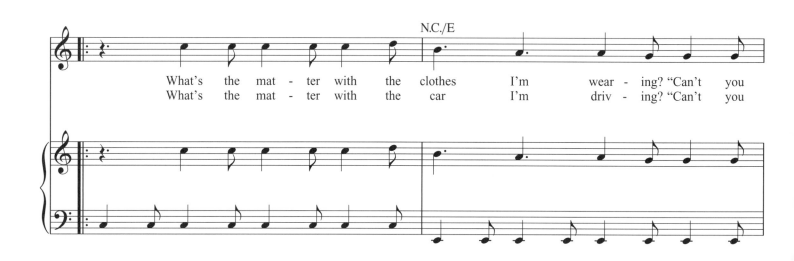

What's the mat-ter with the clothes I'm wear-ing? "Can't you
What's the mat-ter with the car I'm driv-ing? "Can't you

tell that your tie's too wide?" ____
tell that it's out of style?" ____

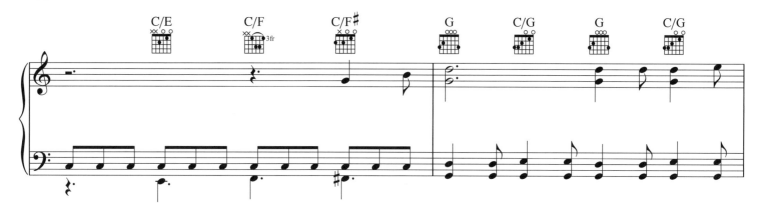

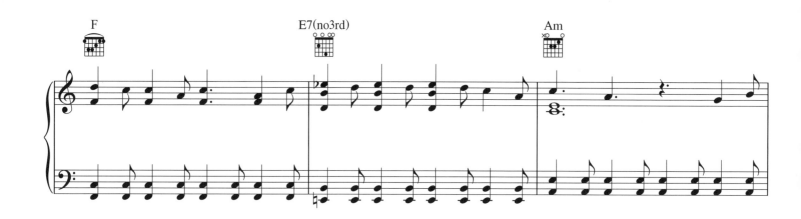

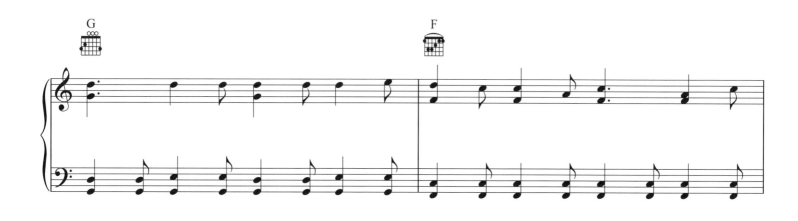

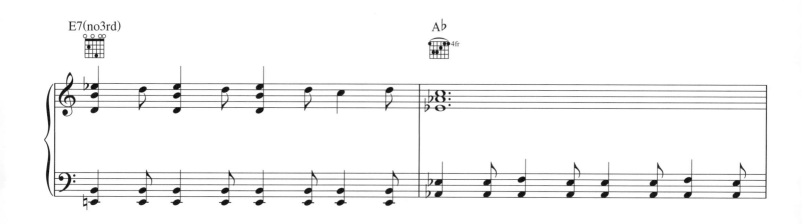

JESSIE'S GIRL

Words and Music by
RICK SPRINGFIELD

JUMP

Words and Music by EDWARD VAN HALEN,
ALEX VAN HALEN and DAVID LEE ROTH

Bright Rock

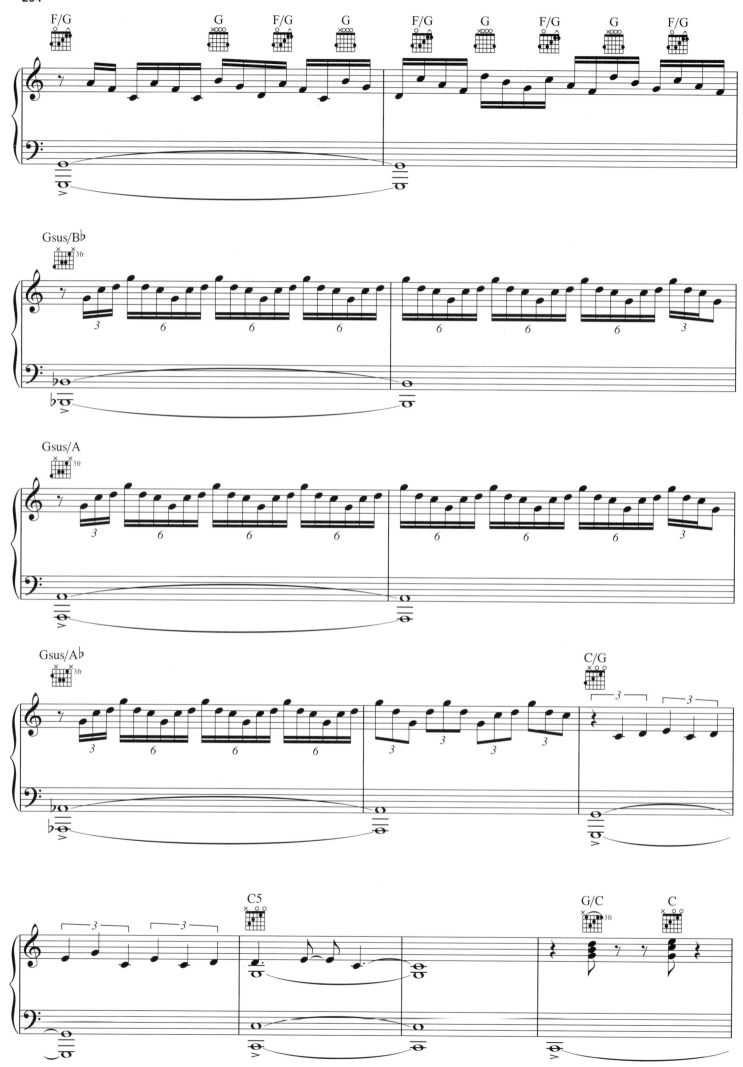

JUST ONCE

Words by CYNTHIA WEIL
Music by BARRY MANN

KARMA CHAMELEON

Words and Music by GEORGE O'DOWD,
JON MOSS, MICHAEL CRAIG,
ROY HAY and PHIL PICKETT

KOKOMO
from the Motion Picture COCKTAIL

Words and Music by JOHN PHILLIPS,
TERRY MELCHER, MIKE LOVE
and SCOTT McKENZIE

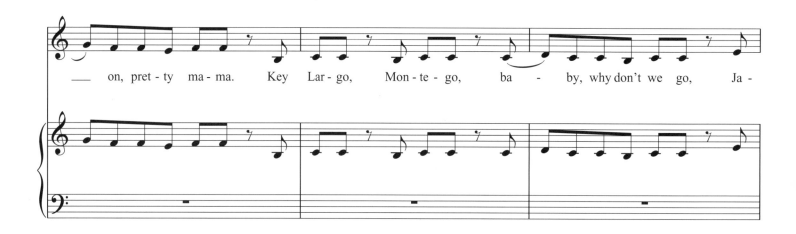

LADY

Words and Music by
LIONEL RICHIE

LET THE DAY BEGIN

Words and Music by
MICHAEL BEEN

Guitar solo ad lib.

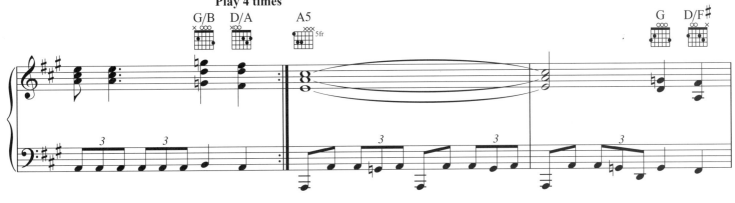

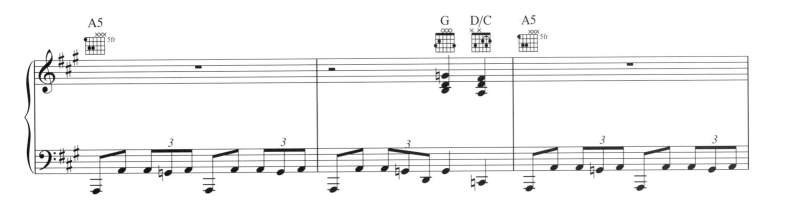

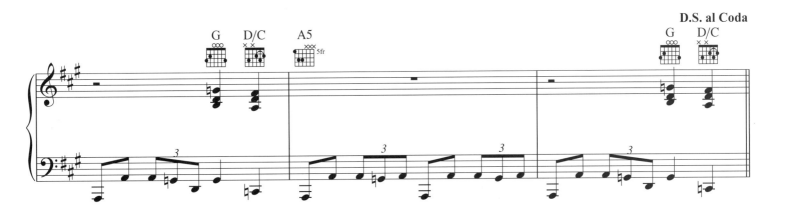

LET'S HEAR IT FOR THE BOY

from the Paramount Motion Picture FOOTLOOSE

Words by DEAN PITCHFORD
Music by TOM SNOW

LIKE A VIRGIN

Words and Music by BILLY STEINBERG
and TOM KELLY

LIVIN' ON A PRAYER

Words and Music by JON BON JOVI,
DESMOND CHILD and RICHIE SAMBORA

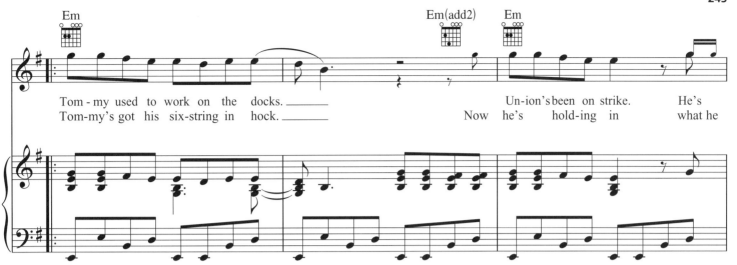

Tom - my used to work on the docks. _____ Un-ion's been on strike. He's
Tom-my's got his six-string in hock. _____ Now he's hold-ing in what he

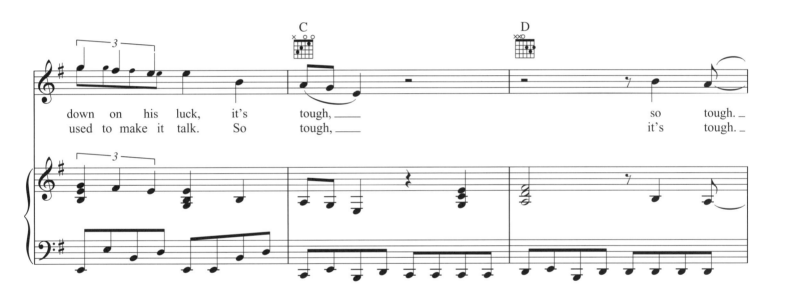

down on his luck, it's tough, _____ so tough. _
used to make it talk. So tough, _____ it's tough. _

Gi - na works the din - er all day. __
Gi - na dreams of run-ning a - way. __

THE LIVING YEARS

Words and Music by MIKE RUTHERFORD
and B.A. ROBERTSON

1. Ev - 'ry gen - er - a - tion _____ blames the one _ be - fore, _
2. crum - pled bits _ of pa - per _____ filled with im - per - fect thought,
3., 4. (*See additional lyrics*)

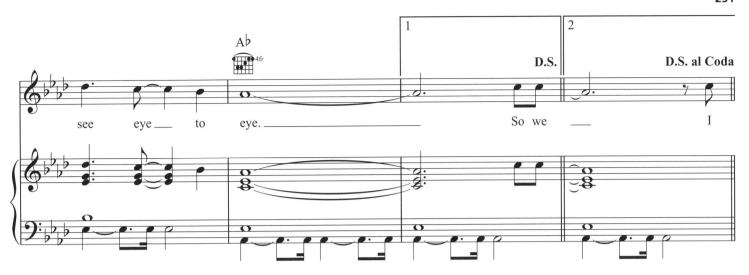

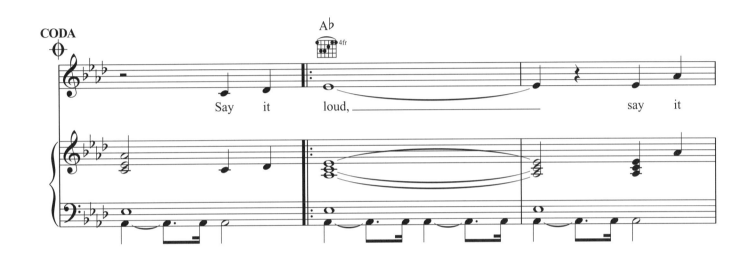

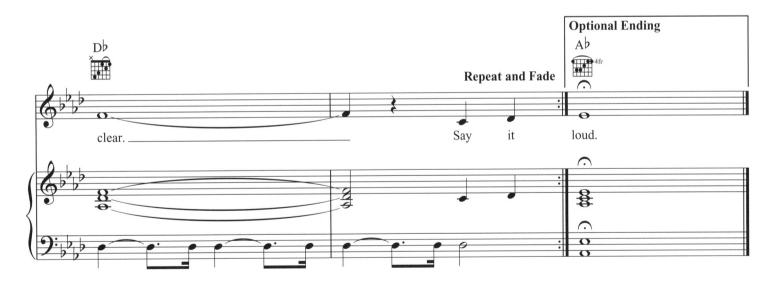

Additional Lyrics

3. So we open up a quarrel
   Between the present and the past.
   We only sacrifice the future.
   It's the bitterness that lasts.
   So don't yield to the fortunes
   You sometimes see as fate.
   It may have a new perspective
   On a different day.
   And if you don't give up
   And don't give in,
   You may just be OK.

4. I wasn't there that morning
   When my father passed away.
   I didn't get to tell him
   All the things I had to say.
   I think I caught his spirit
   Later that same year.
   I'm sure I heard his echo
   In my baby's newborn tears.
   I just wish I could have told him
   In the living years.

LOVE IS A BATTLEFIELD

Words and Music by MIKE CHAPMAN
and HOLLY KNIGHT

(Spoken:) We are young. Heart-ache to heart-ache we stand;

no prom-is-es, no de-mands. Love is a bat-tle-field.

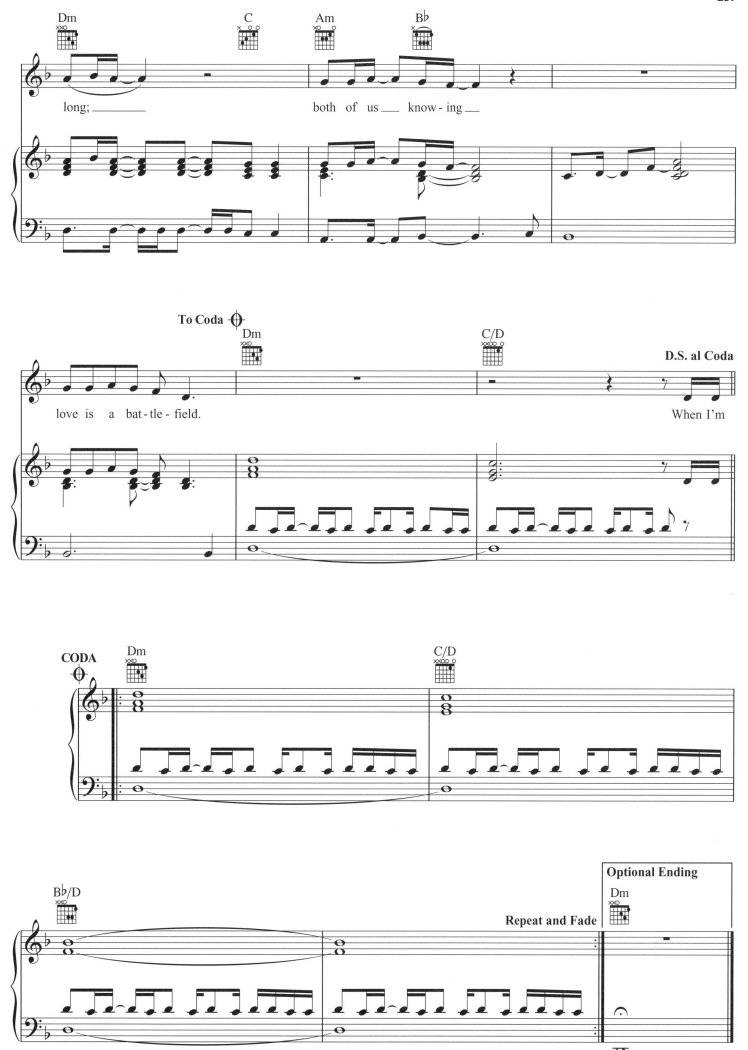

MANEATER

Words by SARA ALLEN,
DARYL HALL and JOHN OATES
Music by DARYL HALL
and JOHN OATES

Oh, ___ here she comes. ___
(Lead vocal ad lib.)

Watch out, boy, ___ she'll chew you up.

MISSING YOU

Words and Music by JOHN WAITE,
CHARLES SANFORD and MARK LEONARD

NINE TO FIVE

Words and Music by
DOLLY PARTON

Tumble out of bed and stumble to the kitchen; pour myself a cup
They let you dream just to watch them shatter; you're just a step on

of ambition, and yawn, and stretch, and try to come to life.
the bossman's ladder, but you've got dreams he'll never take away.

Jump in the shower, and the blood starts pumping;
In the same boat with a lot of your friends,

NOTHING'S GONNA STOP US NOW

Words and Music by DIANE WARREN
and ALBERT HAMMOND

NIGHTSHIFT

Words and Music by WALTER ORANGE,
DENNIS LAMBERT and FRANNE GOLDE

THE ONE I LOVE

Words and Music by WILLIAM BERRY,
PETER BUCK, MICHAEL MILLS
and MICHAEL STIPE

ONE MORE NIGHT

Words and Music by
PHIL COLLINS

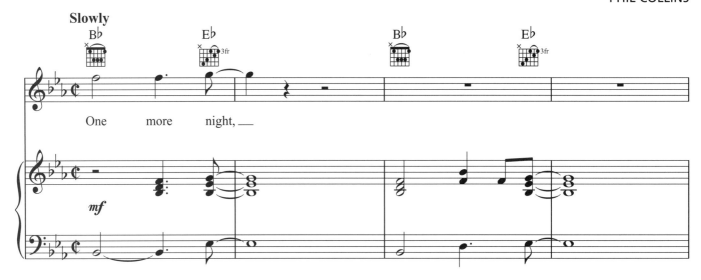

One more night, ___

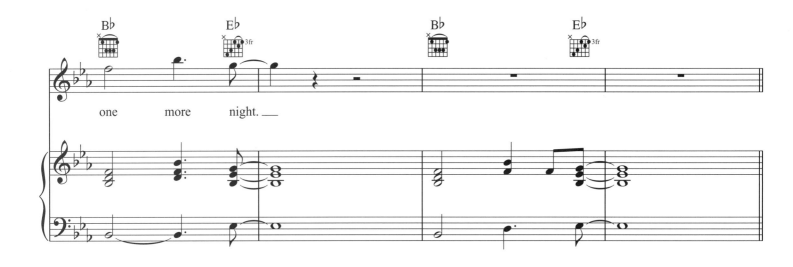

one more night. ___

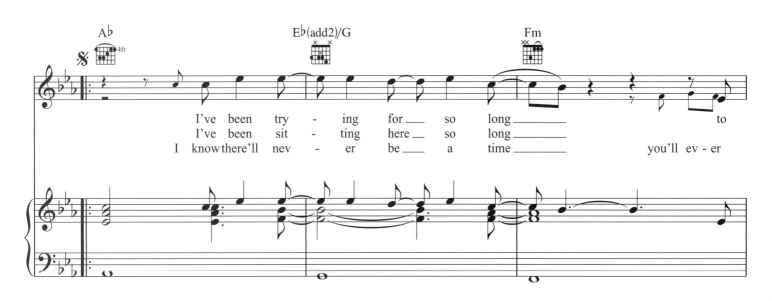

I've been try - ing for ___ so long ___ to
I've been sit - ting here ___ so long ___
I know there'll nev - er be ___ a time ___ you'll ev - er

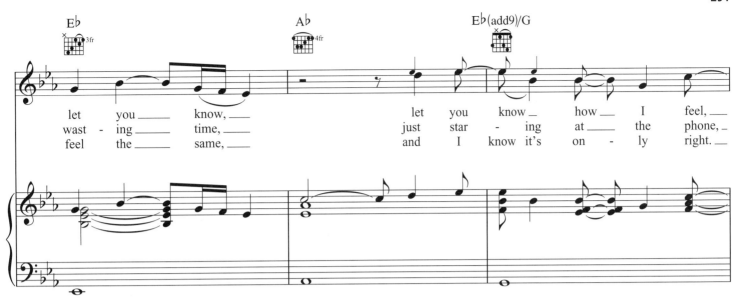

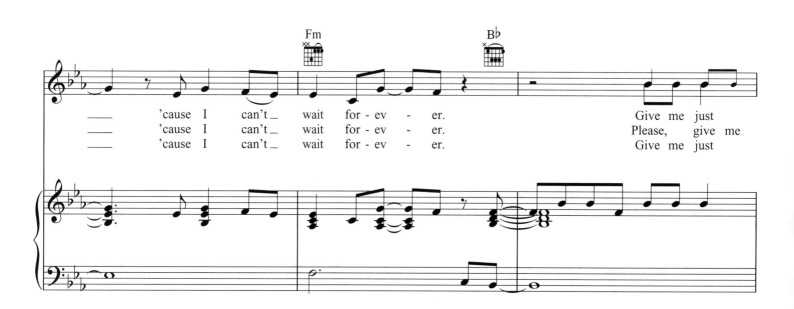

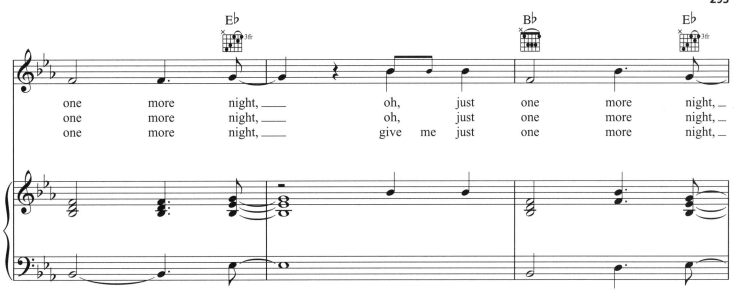

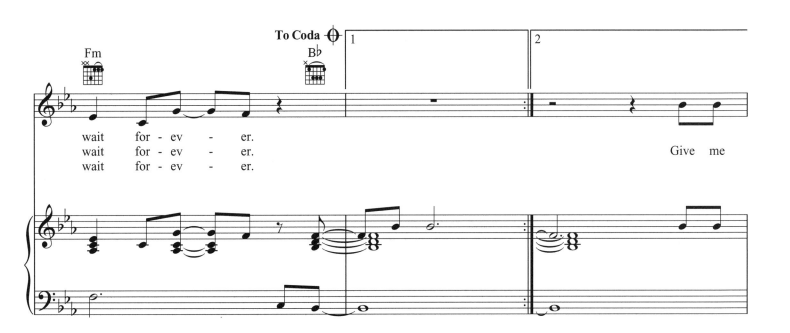

POUR SOME SUGAR ON ME

Words and Music by JOE ELLIOTT, PHIL COLLEN,
RICHARD SAVAGE, RICHARD ALLEN,
STEVE CLARK and R.J. LANGE

Lis - ten:

from my head   to my   feet, _ yeah.

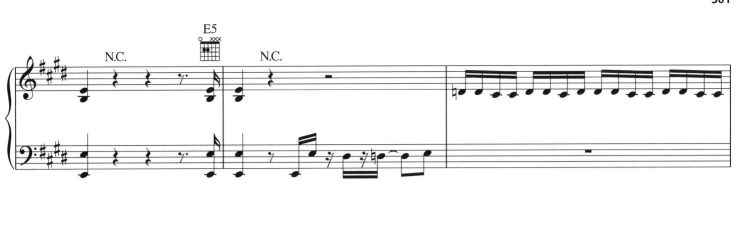

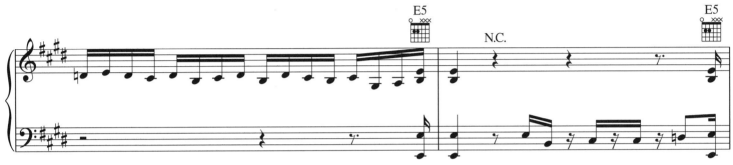

(You got the peach - es, I ____ got the cream.)

Sweet to taste; _ (sac - cha - rine.) _ 'Cause I'm hot, so hot, stick - y sweet, _ from my

(hot, hot, sweet, _

PHYSICAL

Words and Music by STEPHEN A. KIPNER
and TERRY SHADDICK

RIGHT HERE WAITING

Words and Music by
RICHARD MARX

O-ceans a-part,_____ day af-ter day,_____ and I
I took for grant - ed all the times_____ that I

SAILING

Words and Music by
CHRISTOPHER CROSS

SARA

Music by PETER WOLF and INA WOLF
Words by INA WOLF

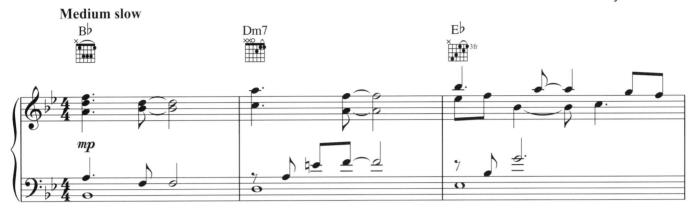

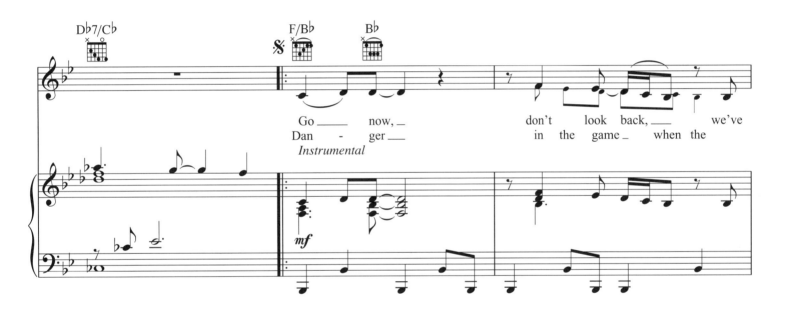

Go ___ now, ___ don't look back, ___ we've
Dan - ger ___ in the game ___ when the
Instrumental

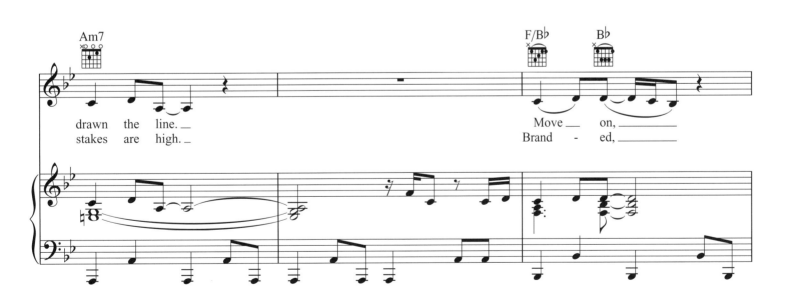

drawn the line. ___ Move ___ on, ___
stakes are high. ___ Brand - ed, ___

SAVING ALL MY LOVE FOR YOU

Words by GERRY GOFFIN
Music by MICHAEL MASSER

few _____ sto - len mo - ments _____ is all _____ that we share.
not _____ ver - y eas - y _____ liv - ing all a - lone. My

You've _____ got your fam - 'ly _____ and they _____ need you there. _____ Though I
friends _____ try and tell me _____ find a man _____ of my own. _____ But _____

SAY SAY SAY

Words and Music by PAUL McCARTNEY
and MICHAEL JACKSON

Say, say, — say _____ what you want but don't play _____ games
go, go, — go _____ where you want but don't leave _____ me
You, you, — you _____ can nev-er say that I'm not _____ the one

with my af-fec- tion. Take, take, — take _____ what you need but
here for-ev- er. You, you, — you _____ stay a-way, so
who real-ly loves_ you. I pray, pray, — pray _____ ev-'ry day that

stand to hear my plead - ing for you, dear? You know I'm cry - ing,
all my tears, ba - by, through the years, you know I'm cry - ing,
all my tears, ba - by, through the years, you know I'm cry - ing,

ooh ooh ooh ooh ooh.

Now ooh.

ain't real, _____ just look at my face, these tears ain't dry-ing.

ooh.

SEPARATE LIVES
Love Theme from WHITE NIGHTS

Words and Music by
STEPHEN BISHOP

Male: You called me from the room in your ho- tel,

all full of ro-mance for some-one that you met,

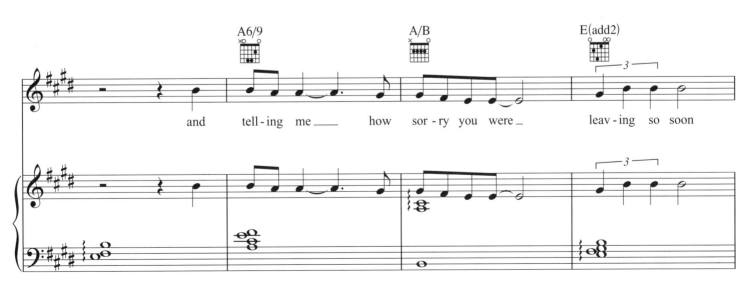

and tell-ing me how sor-ry you were leav-ing so soon

SHE DRIVES ME CRAZY

Words and Music by DAVID STEELE
and ROLAND GIFT

Lyrics:

I can't stop ____
I can't get ____

the way I feel. ____
an - y rest. ____

SISTER CHRISTIAN

Words and Music by
KELLY KEAGY

Moderate Rock

Sis - ter Chris - tian, oh, the
Babe, you know you're grow-ing

time has come, _____ and you know that you're _ the on - ly one _ to say _
up so fast _____ and mom-ma's wor-ry-ing _____ that you won't last to say _

_____ O. K. _____
let's play. _____

Where you go-ing what _ you
Sis - ter Chris-tian, there's _ so

SOMEWHERE OUT THERE

from AN AMERICAN TAIL

Music by BARRY MANN and JAMES HORNER
Lyric by CYNTHIA WEIL

SWEET CHILD O' MINE

Words and Music by W. AXL ROSE,
SLASH, IZZY STRADLIN',
DUFF McKAGAN and STEVEN ADLER

Medium Rock

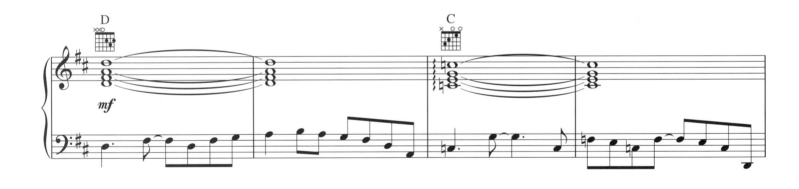

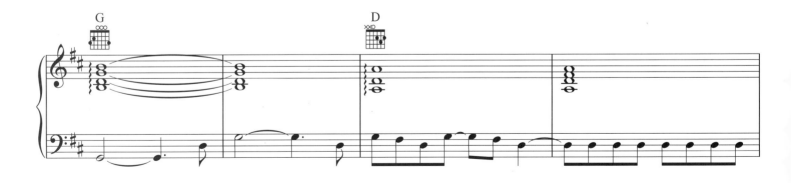

Whoa, oh, oh, oh,

sweet love o' mine.

To Coda

D.S. al Coda

TAKE MY BREATH AWAY
(Love Theme)
from the Paramount Picture TOP GUN

Words and Music by GIORGIO MORODER
and TOM WHITLOCK

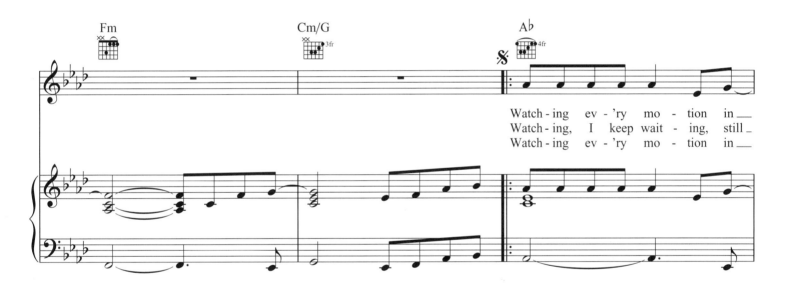

Watch-ing ev-'ry mo-tion in ___
Watch-ing, I keep wait-ing, still ___
Watch-ing ev-'ry mo-tion in ___

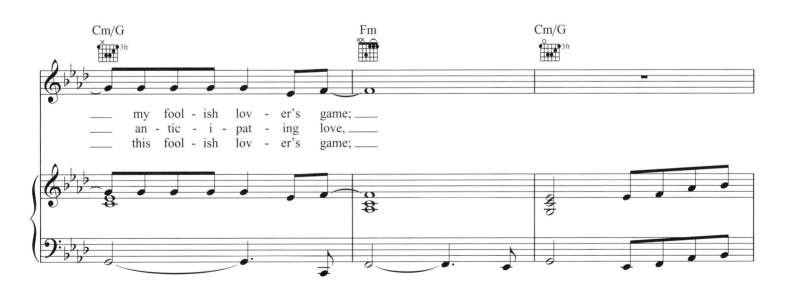

___ my fool-ish lov-er's game; ___
___ an-tic-i-pat-ing love, ___
___ this fool-ish lov-er's game; ___

on this end-less o-cean, fi — n'lly lov-ers know no shame._____
nev-er hes-i-tat-ing to_____ be-come the fat-ed ones._____
haunt-ed by the no-tion some — where there's a love in flames._____

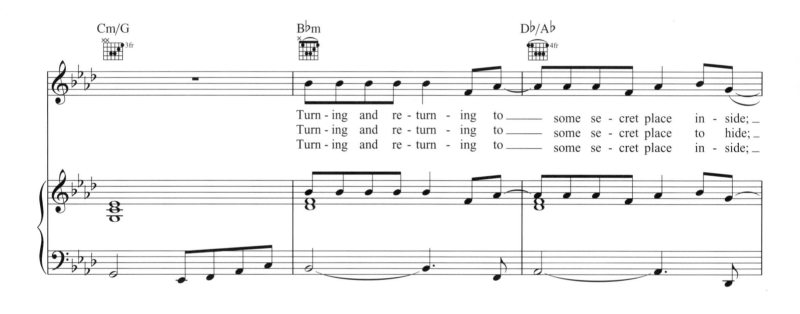

Turn-ing and re-turn-ing to_____ some se-cret place in-side; _
Turn-ing and re-turn-ing to_____ some se-cret place to hide; _
Turn-ing and re-turn-ing to_____ some se-cret place in-side; _

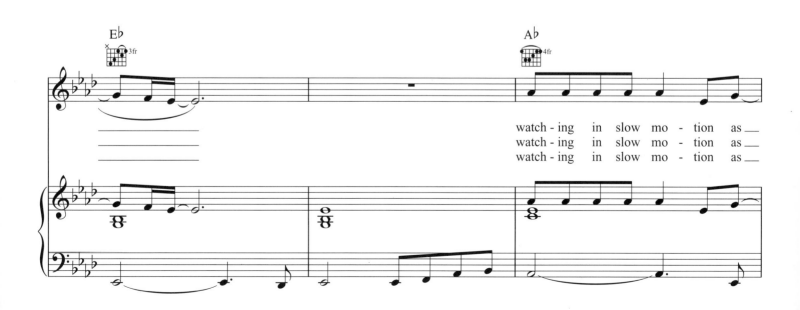

_____
_____
_____

watch-ing in slow mo-tion as_____
watch-ing in slow mo-tion as_____
watch-ing in slow mo-tion as_____

SWEET DREAMS
(Are Made of This)

Words and Music by ANNIE LENNOX
and DAVID STEWART

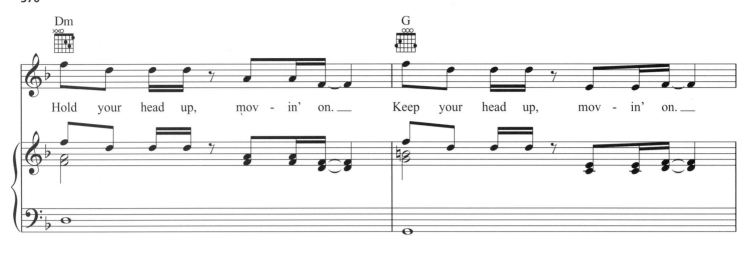

Hold your head up, mov - in' on.___ Keep your head up, mov - in' on.___

Hold your head up, mov - in' on.___ Keep your head up, mov - in' on.___

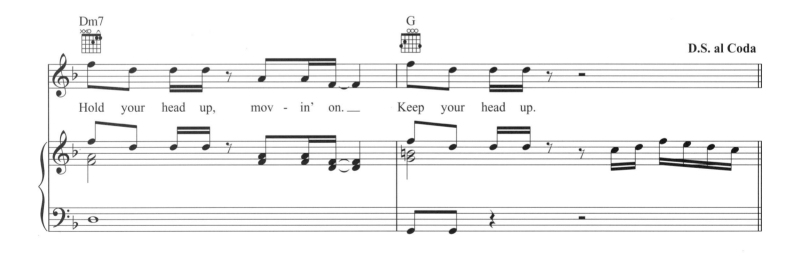

D.S. al Coda

Hold your head up, mov - in' on.___ Keep your head up.

TAKE ON ME

Music by PAL WAAKTAAR and MAGNE FURUHOLMNE
Words by PAL WAAKTAAR,
MAGNE FURUHOLMNE and MORTON HARKET

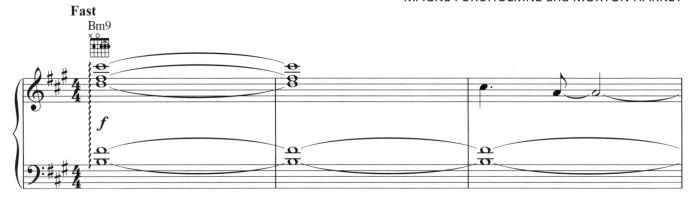

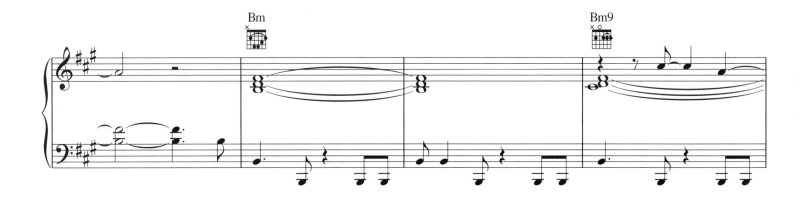

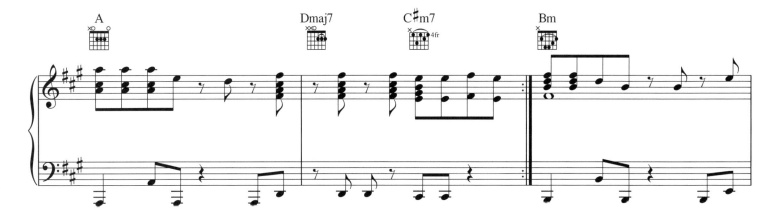

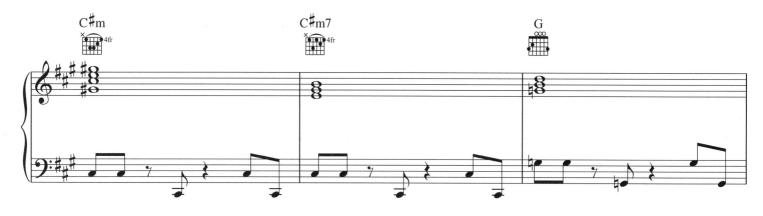

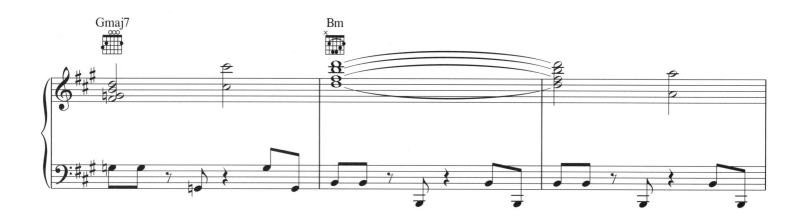

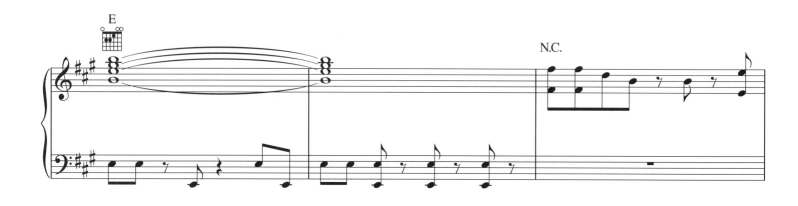

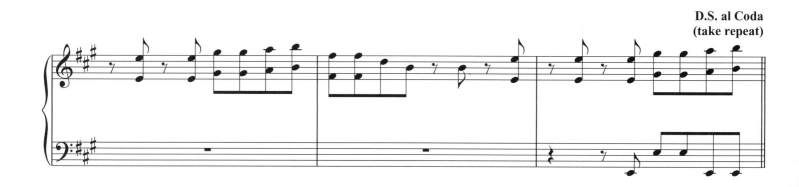

UPSIDE DOWN

Words and Music by NILE RODGERS
and BERNARD EDWARDS

THESE DREAMS

Words and Music by MARTIN GEORGE PAGE
and BERNIE TAUPIN

THROUGH THE YEARS

Words and Music by STEVE DORFF
and MARTY PANZER

TIME AFTER TIME

Words and Music by CYNDI LAUPER
and ROB HYMAN

TRUE COLORS

Words and Music by BILLY STEINBERG
and TOM KELLY

true col - ors are beau - ti - ful, ooh, __ like a rain - bow.

Show me your

rain - bow.

TRULY

Words and Music by
LIONEL RICHIE

UP WHERE WE BELONG

from the Paramount Picture AN OFFICER AND A GENTLEMAN

Words by WILL JENNINGS
Music by BUFFY SAINTE-MARIE and JACK NITZSCHE

A VIEW TO KILL

from A VIEW TO A KILL

Words and Music by JOHN BARRY
and DURAN DURAN

1. Meet-ing you__
2. *See additional lyrics*

with a view__ to a kill,__

face to face,__ in se-cret plac-es,__ feel the chill.

Additional Lyrics

2. Choice for you is the view to a kill.
   Between the shades, assassination standing still.
   The first crystal tears
   Fall as snowflakes on your body.
   First time in years,
   To drench your skin with lovers' rosy stain.
   A chance to find a phoenix for the flame,
   A chance to die, but can we...
   Chorus

THE WAY IT IS

Words and Music by
BRUCE HORNSBY

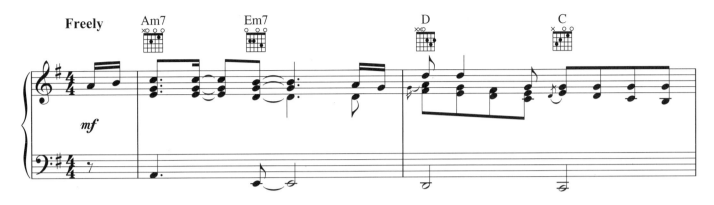

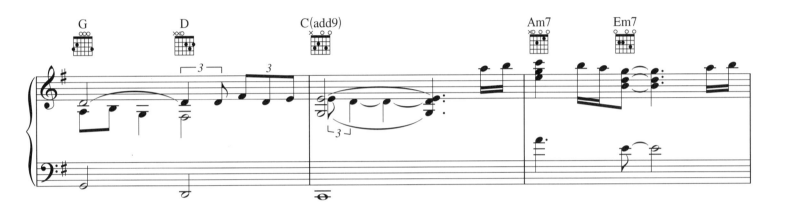

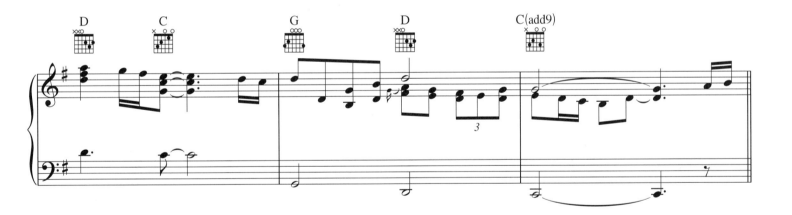

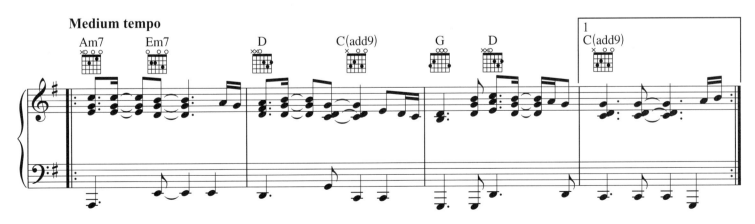

418

WE'RE NOT GONNA TAKE IT

Words and Music by
DANIEL DEE SNIDER

Fast Rock

We're not gon - na take ___ it. No, we ain't gon - na take ___

___ it. We're not gon - na take ___ it an - y - more.

WHAT'S LOVE GOT TO DO WITH IT

Words and Music by TERRY BRITTEN
and GRAHAM LYLE

Slow Rock

You must un-der-stand, though the touch of ___ your hand ___ makes my
may seem to you ___ that I'm act-ing ___ con-fused ___ when you're

pulse re - act, ___
close to ___ me. ___
that it's on-ly ___ the thrill ___ of
If I tend to ___ look dazed, ___ I

boy meet-ing girl, ___ op-po-sites at - tract. ___ It's
read it ___ some-place, ___ I got cause to ___ be. ___ There's a

WITH OR WITHOUT YOU

Words and Music by U2

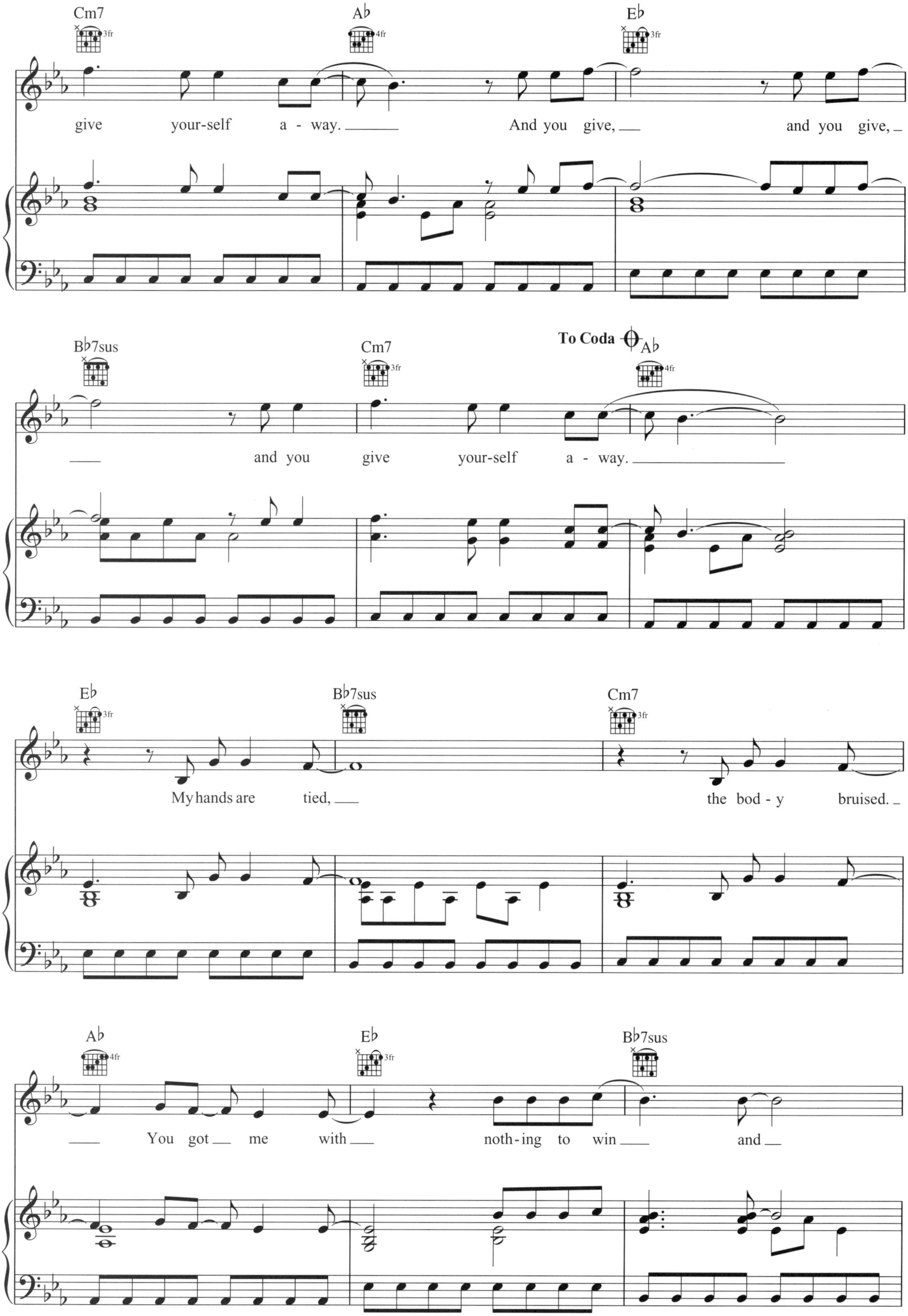

WHEN DOVES CRY

Words and Music by
PRINCE

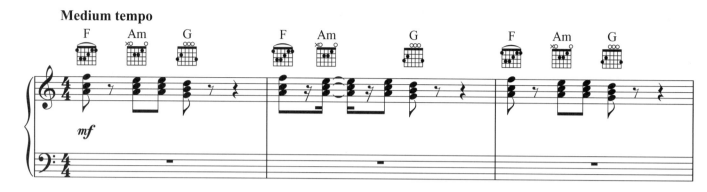

Dig, if U will, __ the pic - ture of

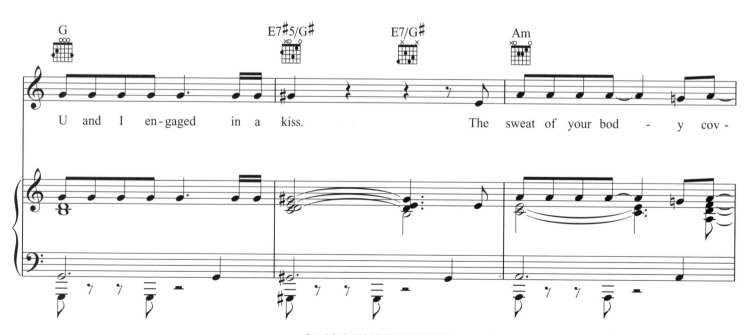

U and I en - gaged in a kiss. The sweat of your bod - y cov-

THE WIND BENEATH MY WINGS
from the Original Motion Picture BEACHES

Words and Music by LARRY HENLEY
and JEFF SILBAR

THE NEW DECADE SERIES

Books with Online Audio • Arranged for Piano, Voice, and Guitar

The New Decade Series features collections of iconic songs from each decade with great backing tracks so you can play them and sound like a pro. You access the tracks online for streaming or download. **See complete song listings online at www.halleonard.com**

SONGS OF THE 1920s
Ain't Misbehavin' • Baby Face • California, Here I Come • Fascinating Rhythm • I Wanna Be Loved by You • It Had to Be You • Mack the Knife • Ol' Man River • Puttin' on the Ritz • Rhapsody in Blue • Someone to Watch over Me • Tea for Two • Who's Sorry Now • and more.
00137576 P/V/G........................$24.99

SONGS OF THE 1930s
As Time Goes By • Blue Moon • Cheek to Cheek • Embraceable You • A Fine Romance • Georgia on My Mind • I Only Have Eyes for You • The Lady Is a Tramp • On the Sunny Side of the Street • Over the Rainbow • Pennies from Heaven • Stormy Weather (Keeps Rainin' All the Time) • The Way You Look Tonight • and more.
00137579 P/V/G........................$24.99

SONGS OF THE 1940s
At Last • Boogie Woogie Bugle Boy • Don't Get Around Much Anymore • God Bless' the Child • How High the Moon • It Could Happen to You • La Vie En Rose (Take Me to Your Heart Again) • Route 66 • Sentimental Journey • The Trolley Song • You'd Be So Nice to Come Home To • Zip-A-Dee-Doo-Dah • and more.
00137582 P/V/G........................$24.99

SONGS OF THE 1950s
Ain't That a Shame • Be-Bop-A-Lula • Chantilly Lace • Earth Angel • Fever • Great Balls of Fire • Love Me Tender • Mona Lisa • Peggy Sue • Que Sera, Sera (Whatever Will Be, Will Be) • Rock Around the Clock • Sixteen Tons • A Teenager in Love • That'll Be the Day • Unchained Melody • Volare • You Send Me • Your Cheatin' Heart • and more.
00137595 P/V/G........................$24.99

SONGS OF THE 1960s
All You Need Is Love • Beyond the Sea • Born to Be Wild • California Girls • Dancing in the Street • Happy Together • King of the Road • Leaving on a Jet Plane • Louie, Louie • My Generation • Oh, Pretty Woman • Sunshine of Your Love • Under the Boardwalk • You Really Got Me • and more.
00137596 P/V/G.....................$24.99

SONGS OF THE 1970s
ABC • Bridge over Troubled Water • Cat's in the Cradle • Dancing Queen • Free Bird • Goodbye Yellow Brick Road • Hotel California • I Will Survive • Joy to the World • Killing Me Softly with His Song • Layla • Let It Be • Piano Man • The Rainbow Connection • Stairway to Heaven • The Way We Were • Your Song • and more.
00137599 P/V/G $27.99

SONGS OF THE 1980s
Africa • Beat It • Careless Whisper • Come on Eileen • Don't Stop Believin' • Every Rose Has Its Thorn • Footloose • I Just Called to Say I Love You • Jessie's Girl • Livin' on a Prayer • Saving All My Love for You • Take on Me • Up Where We Belong • The Wind Beneath My Wings • and more.
00137600 P/V/G.......................$27.99

SONGS OF THE 1990s
Angel • Black Velvet • Can You Feel the Love Tonight • (Everything I Do) I Do It for You • Friends in Low Places • Hero • I Will Always Love You • More Than Words • My Heart Will Go On (Love Theme from 'Titanic') • Smells like Teen Spirit • Under the Bridge • Vision of Love • Wonderwall • and more.
00137601 P/V/G $27.99

SONGS OF THE 2000s
Bad Day • Beautiful • Before He Cheats • Chasing Cars • Chasing Pavements • Drops of Jupiter (Tell Me) • Fireflies • Hey There Delilah • How to Save a Life • I Gotta Feeling • I'm Yours • Just Dance • Love Story • 100 Years • Rehab • Unwritten • You Raise Me Up • and more.
00137608 P/V/G $27.99

HAL•LEONARD® CORPORATION
7777 W. Bluemound Rd. P.O. Box 13819 Milwaukee, WI 53213

halleonard.com
Prices, content, and availability subject to change without notice.

1214